Cody   Danielle   Natalie   Hyeon   Vjollca

Gjurd   Ùisdean   Patricia   Baozhai   Nicole

Hannah   Mykhailo   Umut   Gemma   Frank

Jayden   Rajeshri   Leanne   Lajpal   Pirjo

To Chung Sum Lam. And Karen B. and Karen L.

Text and illustrations © 2021 Thao Lam

Owlkids Books acknowledges the financial support of the Canada Council for the Arts, the Ontario Arts
Council, the Government of Canada through the Canada Book Fund (CBF) and the Government of Ontario
through the Ontario Creates Book Initiative for our publishing activities.

Published in Canada by Owlkids Books Inc., 1 Eglinton Avenue East, Toronto, ON M4P 3A1
Published in the US by Owlkids Books Inc., 1700 Fourth Street, Berkeley, CA 94710

Library of Congress Control Number: 2020941424

Library and Archives Canada Cataloguing in Publication

Title: Thao / by Thao Lam.
Names: Lam, Thao, author, illustrator.
Identifiers: Canadiana 2020028570X | ISBN 9781771474320 (hardcover)
Classification: LCC PS8623.A466 T53 2021 | DDC jC813/.6—dc23

Edited by Karen Li and Karen Boersma | Design and handlettering by Alisa Baldwin

Manufactured in Shenzhen, Guangdong, China, in November 2020, by WKT Co. Ltd.
Job #20CB0771

A   B   C   D   E   F

ONTARIO ARTS COUNCIL
CONSEIL DES ARTS DE L'ONTARIO
an Ontario government agency
un organisme du gouvernement de l'Ontario

Canada Council   Conseil des Arts
for the Arts   du Canada

Canadä

 Publisher of Chirp, Chickadee and OWL
www.owlkidsbooks.com | Owlkids Books is a division of bayard canada

THAO

by

Thao Lam

Owlkids Books

It's not easy being Thao.

My name has the same letters as other names.

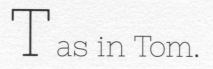

H like Henry.

A for Amy.

O
it would be
so much easier if
my name were
Olivia...

Letters get added, scrambled,
and left behind.

Sigh.

Where did the *L*
come from?

Not. Even. *Close.*

Eventually, I learned to
recognize the names people
gave me.

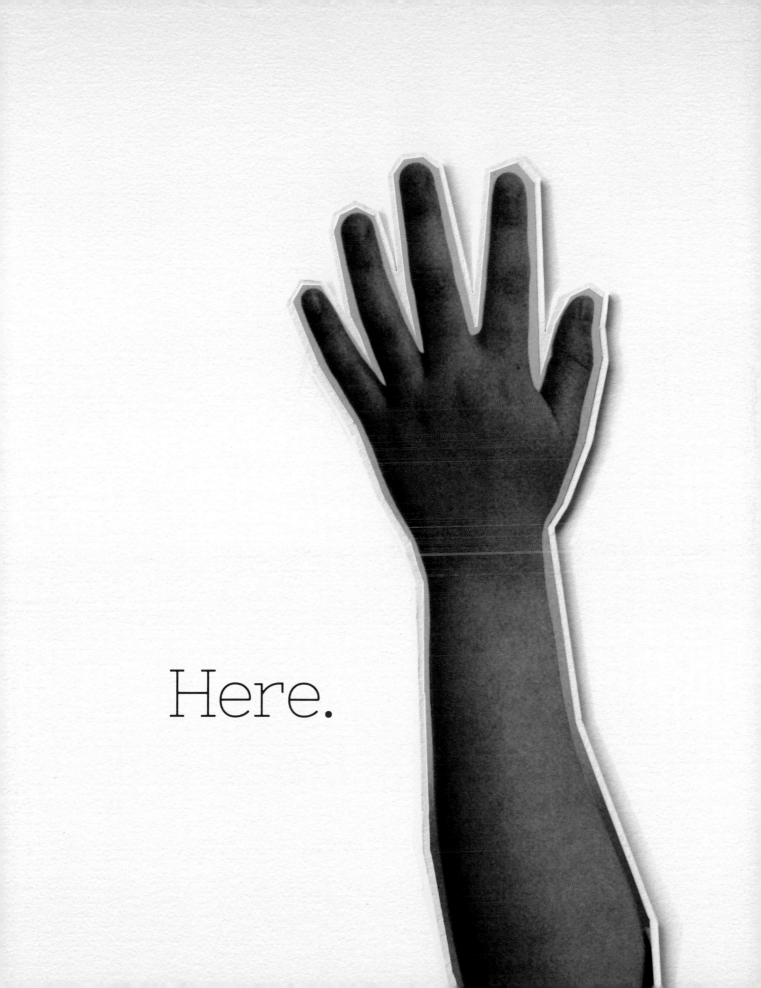

Here.

And there were many of those.

TOFU.

TINY!

CHINA GIRL.

SHRIMP

TOOT TOOT

TWO TAE THAW

Karen, Michael, Melissa, or John—any of
these names would have been easier.

Just call me

Jennifer.

The next day, Jennifer got up in the morning.

Jennifer brushed her teeth.

Jennifer walked to school.

Jennifer asked a zillion questions during science class but spaced out during math.

Jennifer made a mess in art class and sang off-key during music lessons.

For lunch, Jennifer's mom had packed...

Gỏi cuốn!

Thao's favorite!

My name is Thao.

It helps if you take out the *H* when you say it. But remember to put it back in when you spell it.

Thao Hong Lam.

Not that kind of

lamb!

Nicholas

Ian

Rafiki

Alisa

Unnur

Peter

Crystal

Yu Yan

James

Wendy

Jawaria

Njáll

Kimberly

Floortje

Zachary

Yejide

Gulbahar

Dennis

Awinita

Odhran